I0471444

PLAN, CREATE, OPTIMIZE, DISTRIBUTE!

Your Strategic Roadmap to Content Marketing Success

GABRIELA TAYLOR

ISBN-13: 978-1490960906
ISBN-10: 1490960902

Legal Notice

The publisher and author have strived to be as accurate and complete as possible in the creation of this book. The contents within are accurate and up to date at the time of writing however the publisher accepts that due to the rapidly changing nature of the Internet some information may not be fully up to date at the time of reading.

Whilst all attempts have been made to verify information provided in this publication, the Publisher assumes no responsibility for errors, omissions, or contrary interpretation of the subject matter herein. Any perceived slights of specific people or organizations are unintentional.

All Rights Reserved

CONTENTS

INTRODUCTION – FROM INTERRUPTION MARKETING TO ENGAGEMENT MARKETING

Engagement marketing is not a new concept. However, the evolving marketplace and the growing prominence of Web 2.0 platforms means that engagement marketing has come to the forefront in today's marketing efforts. Engagement marketing is a move from one-way campaigns to a strategy that seeks to have dialogue with the customer. Unlike traditional forms of marketing that bombard and interrupt the customer, engagement marketing leverages the specific needs of the customer. It is also about encouraging customers to interact among themselves, which can build advocacy for your brand.

Essentially, engagement marketing attempts to merge traditional media with contemporary marketing tools such as social media, web communities, virtual events and mobile technology. So how do you go about bringing the customer to the center of your marketing campaign?

Connect with the customer on a personal level
Customers are looking for brands that are targeting and meeting their needs. Instead of blasting out messages to

1

everyone, a marketer must find out who their target audience is and evaluate their interests.

Social media and online communities have made this possible without the need for a large needs assessment budget. Looking at what people are saying, their social interactions, and the type of questions they are asking online is a good starting point to understand their needs.

Build a content relationship

Today, tools such as blogs and social forums have freed up the flow and accessibility of information from the minority to the majority. Customers are looking for content that interests them and compels them toward a certain action. Investing in content creation is necessary for the marketer who is looking to move toward customer engagement. The content you send out should also be targeted, informative and entertaining.

Call your audience to action

This step is at the heart of engagement marketing. Instead of your campaign being about you sending out one-way messages, a call-to-action encourages your audience to jump in and participate. You are saying to them that their input is valued. Calls-to-action including asking your audience to share content they find interesting on your website or blog, for example. Social media has made this more possible than ever and Internet users are able to share content with their network much faster. Calls-to-action allow your target audience to do the marketing for you; this creates even greater trust around your brand.

Provide a platform for customer feedback

Encourage readers to leave comments and to discuss among themselves. Encourage guest posts as well as suggestions that readers might have. Be sure to respond to feedback and to engage your audience for example, by asking questions that will trigger a conversation. As part of your customer feedback strategy, conduct frequent polls around a certain matter to see what customers think and what they might be looking for that you are currently not offering. Again, web tools have made online marketing easier and less costly.

Throughout this book I will cover some of the best strategies in content marketing including areas such as content planning, content creation, content optimization, and content distribution. You'll also learn the different types of content, the pros and cons of free and paid content or the difference between content creation and content curation. That's just few of the things you will learn from this book that will conclude with a section on content performance measurement that will show you the diverse metrics and tools that you can use to determine how well you are achieving your content market goals.

1
FREE VS. PREMIUM

Content marketing is a vital aspect of lead generation. This entails the creation and distributions of valuable information to introduce an audience to a brand, a product or service. At a time when users are eager for informative content, marketers are left to determine whether they should offer their content free or place a pay wall and limit access to this information only to those who pay for it. Here are some considerations to take with regard to free and premium models of content marketing:

Profits
It seems counterintuitive to be in business only to give out things free. When it comes to content marketing there is a difference in what free and paid mean. Paid does not always entails payment with money and credit cards. It can also mean paying by providing personal information such as a user's name and their email address. On a purely monetary basis, the premium model is more profitable than the 'freemium' one. Membership sites that require users to pay a

certain monthly or annual fee to access content are some of the most profitable models today.

Lead Generation

Lead generation is at the heart of content marketing. Free models for content marketing have been seen to be the most helpful in lead generation in the long term. This is especially applicable for content downloads such as ebooks; users are more likely to download a free ebook than they are one that requires monetary payment or personal information. However, the downside to this is that a marketer would have to look for other strategies to obtain users' personal information.

Trust

Businesses, especially those operating online are working in a low-trust environment. This means that before people buy anything or offer their information, they need to trust you first. Offering free access to content is one way to build trust. This is why the 'freemium' model is a long-term lead-generation strategy rather than an immediate one. If you offer valuable and expert information, users will be more willing to give you their information; in this way, they will be paying with their personal information to access your content. They will also be more inclined to make monetary payments if they find your content is very valuable to them. Paid content can struggle with this regard, as users are less trusting of online businesses that ask them to pay upfront, even if the information might be valuable.

Shareable

Free content is more sharable than paid content. If you are looking for a greater audience to read your content, then the 'freemium' model may be more beneficial. This is especially true for videos content and for ebooks. The viral nature of social media has made it possible for marketers to have millions of users read their content. This can be a great way of attracting traffic, after which you can develop a strategy for creating a strong customer base for your content and products.

2

27 CONTENT TYPES THAT EVERY MARKETER OUGHT TO TRY

There are many types of content you can post online and in this chapter I would like to introduce you to some of the most used types. When you market online, content is the key to everything. It brings traffic to your site, it entertains and informs your customers making them return to your site, and it converts potential customers into sales.

1. Lists

Lists have become popular among blog authors and readers. They include tools, resources and tips. Formulating a 'Best of', 'Top 10 worst' or a 'Top 5' is a simple task regardless of the subject. Lists make the blog posts look organized.

2. News

Entails dissemination of any industry-related news or niche like company closing and opening, special events or management shake-ups.

3. Questions And Answers Posts

Distribute practical or thought-provoking questions to the readers. Invite them to provide answers through your blog's comment section. You must respond to these comments before giving the answer.

You can also create posts that provide answers to your readers' frequently asked questions (FAQs) or those on message boards and social media.

4. Checklists

Requires writing printable lists concerning steps to complete an action.

5. How-to Guides

You can enlighten your blog readers with step-by-step guides to undertaking certain tasks. An example is 'How to wash a cardigan'.

6. Surveys And Polls

This strategy entails asking questions. A poll consists of a question with various possible answers. A survey is a questionnaire that contains several simple fill-in-the-blanks, poll-styled and essay questions. You can find a suitable plugin for polls and surveys by searching your WordPress plugin directory. Both, polls and surveys are valuable sources of information regarding your audience.

7. Interviews

Many people have been able to share their success stories, from celebrities, experts, and ordinary successful people to companies and other bloggers. There are varieties of means used to conduct interviews such as the traditional method, whereby meetings are conducted in person. They are also conducted through email, Skype, Tweeter, or phone.

Skype's best feature is 'Screen Sharing' that allows computer screens sharing among people on different ends of a video call. It's ideal in giving presentations remotely, showing codes to other programmers and displaying the current content in your browser. Skype supports group messaging, video and audio conference calls. Through its 'Add People' command, you can add others in the above menu. While engaging in audio conversation, the 'Add People' command incorporates the desired contacts into the call. While texting or talking, you can share photos and files.

8. Slideshows

Effective slideshows should move quickly, enabling the user to consume the main theme in less than 3 seconds. With the presentation content laid out, the next step is designing. Large, vibrant, and engaging designs compliment and emphasize on the main point. Text has to be featured in the designs and the words should be used in moderation; a handful of words with vivid imagery has great effect.

9. Webinars

These are interactive tools used for sales and training especially when geographic location poses a hindrance. They allow the users to interact through audio and video conferencing facilities and share information through transmission of data formats such as images and word documents.

Things to remember when setting up for a webinar:

a) An introductory slide guiding the audience on the tools they require for the webinar where and how to obtain them and the starting time of the webinar.

b) An informative slide of the presenters' profile and their relevance on the topics, job titles and possibly a photograph for their profile.

c) An overview of the webinar's objectives and areas of coverage during discussion.

d) Slides relevant to the subject of discussion.

There are, however, webinar tools that enable real-time display of your interaction with data on your computer. You can browse for appropriate softwares that meet your needs online from numerous sites. Examples of these include *IdealWare, TechSoup, ReadyTalk* and *GoToWebinar*.

After recording the webinar video or slides you should then share them through the available media. Such may include posting links online on social sites such as Facebook, on the company website or through emails.

10. Case Studies

Small business owners can create perfect case studies using several strategies. First, you must unearth your intended segment or demographic group. This helps in formulating appealing content.

<u>Creating a case study:</u>

Discovery Work

You must recognize your target audience's challenges, the causal issues and possible solutions. List all the possible solutions while analyzing your competitors' efficiency in solving the same challenges.

Select A Relevant Subject

Select issues related to industry events or news to capture readership. This forms the case study's main pillar.

Objectives Identification

You must set your goals including constructing brand awareness, earning media coverage, driving leads and increasing website traffic.

Researching Priority Keywords

The next step involves the selection of priority keywords. Using tools like *Google's Keyword Tool*, you can discover the most prominent keywords related to your audience's problem.

11. Animated GIF images

Animated GIF images can pull a lot of attention to your site. They are creative banner ads that are also very funny. Memorializing favorite movie scenes using the GIF format has gained widespread popularity.

Tools to use:

Photoshop: Using Photoshop (at least versions CS3), you can easily have your own animated GIF. You only need a 72 pixel-per-inch resolution for your web display. You must drag all the personal image file 'cells' into Photoshop. They will then stack up in the same image. You can also access videos in MP4, MPEG, MOV and AVI formats through Photoshop. The animated GIF must be fast - you can achieve this by selecting few frames by selecting 'Range to Import'. Photoshop imports these frames in a layer format. You must reconvert them to frames by resizing and cropping them.

Picasion.com: Picasion.com is free and allows you to upload individual photos for the creation of animated GIFs. Remember to align them in the same dimensions. Sources of these photos include URLs, Picassa or Flickr. Your webcam can also suffice in creating your personal animation.

However, you must set its speed at a faster tempo and its size to 400 pixels. Still, you must click on the site to take your individual frame image.

12. Videos

Create current and relevant content. First, understand the goal of your intended video and conduct research on scripting and content. Secondly, identify the appropriate video type that best expresses your content goals. Then, find the best ways to reach the customers. Ensure that the video type selected is graphically stimulating for viewers and informative in terms of the intended message. In this age of content marketing, the marketer should strive to give the consumers information relating to their needs and how best to satisfy them. You should therefore ensure that the video is both interesting and beneficial to the viewer.

Script your video: Strive to ensure that the video captures the audiences' attention in the first 5 seconds of the presentation. Visual aids go a long way in enhancing this effect.

Brand the video: This refers to ensuring that the video compliments the company marketing campaigns through incorporation of the company logo or graphics, marketing messages or advertisement captions.

Tools to use:

Depending on your editing needs, you require a software application that enables you to meet your video quality production needs. For example *Camtasia Studio* is an excellent application for editing video and adding a recorded soundtrack to it while *Instant Demo* is appropriate when you record your own narration.

Upload the videos to online storage providers such as *Amazon S3*. Their CloudFront system enables users access the large content files from most-convenient servers worldwide. All you need to access both these features is to create an account through the Amazon Web Services homepage. To access the video files in S3 you require a flash player, which is a program that runs in your browser to display the video's content. The *JW Player* is a good example of such an application and contains numerous plug-ins while still maintaining a simple and light framework. All you need to do is download the player, install according to the auto-run instructions provided and test it using the sample clip provided.

Video embedding: Post links of videos on your site as the JW player enables you to view the HTML code of the movies. Once posted, the videos are published to the rest of the world for viewing.

13. Memes

A meme is a behavior, idea or concept that mostly spreads through the Internet. They are usually available in visual forms like videos or pictures. Other forms of memes include hashtags, links, phrases, websites, simple misspelled words.

Creating memes is a simple and quick process. It requires basic knowledge of *Photoshop* or *Microsoft Paint*. Nonetheless, you can use numerous other meme generators out there such as *quickmeme* and *MemeGenerator*.

Your meme must relate to your brand or industry. A successful meme must have some semblance to your brand like slogan, mission, messaging and industry. Your meme should have humor and entertaining content. Avoid coming off as too serious rather combine your brand identity with a funny or witty tone.

14. Infographics

Infographics offer a quick and powerful avenue for portraying complex ideas to audiences. Popular uses of infographics include clearly communicating the purpose and activities pertaining to programs, visually and aesthetically portraying data, focusing attention on complex matters and visually comparing conflicting design and factors. Basically the more complex a data set is, the more visual aids are required to simplify it.

Infogr.am is an online tool that can be used to create interactive charts and graphs. It uses data on uploaded spreadsheets to plot the charts and modify the previous ones. There are four different chart types that can be produced through the application: bar graphs, pie charts, line graphs and matrix charts. The user only needs to upload data onto his account on the site for manipulation. The information may be viewed when the cursor is hovered over the chart. Charts created on infogr.am can be embedded on websites, blogs and other online forums.

15. Mindmaps

Mindmapping refers to drawing mental images from the acquired ideas. This process facilitates brainstorming whereby people explore the brain for ideas. Although mind mapping can be done on paper, online tools are also available, some of which require neither downloading nor installation. Online mind mapping tools could be either free or paid versions. The majority of such web applications can be used anywhere from any browser.

One of the tools I recommend using to create mindmaps is *Xmind* that features a more professional feel than *FreeMind*. It also has a 'pro' version with several customizable features such as the brainstorming mode.

16. Podcasts

They facilitate the creation of a chunk of audio programming accessed on demand.

Tools to use:

Blogtalkradio

This is a podcast and social networking site featuring simple steps on creating on-demand audio.

PodBean.com

PodBean.com offers three simple steps on publishing your own podcast without a technology curve. You can as well share your podcast on Facebook, Blogger, MySpace, among other sites.

PodOmatic

PodOmatic offers two options: Basic and Pro. Basic features 500MB storage, easy tools, and 15GB of bandwidth monthly. Pro incorporates more features for about $10 monthly. More information is available at the PodOmatic website.

<u>Below there is an outline of the simple process of recording a podcast:</u>

a) Plug a microphone into a computer.

b) Install an audio recorder for your operating system: Window, Mac, or Linux. *Audacity, Easy Record V5* and *Record for All* are free software for audio recorders.

c) Make a record by recording music or speech and save it on the computer to produce an audio file.

d) Upload the podcast to either of the podcasting sites (FreeForAll has a tutorial on the uploading process). *FreeForAll* and *Self Seo* offer advice that would guide you in promoting the uploaded podcast.

17. Press Releases

Current press releases feature larger audiences from customers to investors. The language and terminologies used should hence be widely accessible, without overestimating the audience's level of knowledge in the field. Simple questions like who or what, should all be answered in the story.

What Should You Include in Your Press Release?

The press release should engage the audience. Supporting media should hence be incorporated whenever necessary, to help customers understand the content. Popular daily events and interesting texts should be included. Featuring photos, quotes, and videos in the story would capture the readers' interest. Press releases should include information supporting your message like:

a) quotes from key persons like the company president or industry experts

b) customer testimonials

c) product reviews

d) awards and other important recognitions

e) offers or calls-to-action

Marketing claims should be supported with evidence. In order to claim of the 'best product', you should include third party reviews or specifications. State how hiring a new employee or winning an award, would influence your business, together with the benefit it offers to the clients.

Hyperlinks: They link key phrases and calls-to-action to the appropriate landing pages on your web site. They also facilitate order placements or sign up by the customers. Links to websites appear wherever press releases are published. The incoming links help with the ranking of search engines for the hyperlinked phrases.

Photos: Photos distinguish ordinary press releases. Photographs of new products and newly hired employees should be included in advertisements.

Audio: The included audio clips may incorporate interview audio clips, podcast excerpts and quotes featured in press releases.

Video: Videos add an extra dimension absent in press releases, featuring product reviews, demonstrations, or interviews.

Social Media Facilities: Adding bookmarking buttons that post on sites like Delicious would popularize the press releases. People expose their friends to your release as they share it or bookmark using social media.

18. Product Pages (Landing Page/Sales Letter)

These pages spotlight products and offer shoppers a 'Buy' button. They should be simple, providing quick access to information sources. Providing very complex information can discourage customers and then they give up on buying due to uncertainty. Successful online merchants attribute their success to focusing each product page on a single product.

Below there are some <u>tips on optimizing your landing page for a better conversion</u>:

a) The heading should directly refer to the visitor's origin or the ad copy that led to the click. Being the most important part of the landing page, the language should be matched as exactly as possible to keep visitors oriented and engaged.

b) Provide a clear call-to-action. The visitors should receive clear direction using graphics, hot-lined texts, or both. Use a minimum of 2 calls of action in a short landing page, 3-5 in a longer one.

c) Write in the second person. This gives visitors better conviction on how the products benefit them.

d) Aim to deliver a clear persuasive message without showing off. The business should not be used as an artistic expression.

19. Digital Newsletters

As communication and marketing tool, digital newsletters fulfill various functions. They are reminders to your users about you, your products, and your latest activities. They also help to forge a relationship with these customers. Email newsletters must contain relevant, fresh and enjoyable information. By signing up for these newsletters, users hope to find information they would not find elsewhere.

Your newsletter must address your readers' important issues. It should be in bullet list or short write-up to enhance easy skimming. Any ad in the newsletter must relate to your field of operation. Furthermore, the ads must not be in excess as it could scare readers away. You can make the newsletter visually appealing through charts, graphics or images. These elements guide them on the most crucial messages or content. Be sure to include numbers like dollar values and percentages. This grabs users' attention since they connect them to savings and prices.

<u>Tools to use:</u>

You can use *Campaign Monitor*, which provides amazing resources and prices. It incurs $5 worth of delivery fee and $0.01 per subscriber. Or you can use *MailChimp* and enjoy great analytics together with a free plan.

20. eBooks and White papers
sBooks

eBooks must have descriptive and interesting titles. This will capture reader interest since it indicates its contents. The title must also be appealing, readable and possibly have images and branding elements.

Adding a table of contents: As it is customary with all books, you must add a clickable table of contents to your eBook. This way, your readers can understand the book's organization and reference certain chapters easily.

Adding social sharing badges on each page is also mandatory. Hence, your readers would easily share it through their social networks regardless of how far they have read. Nevertheless, ensure that you have shared links to your eBook's landing page. Use visual elements to break big chunks of text or copy such as graphs, images, screenshots, headers, bullet points and bolded text.

White papers

White papers are written in the format of special reports but contain persuasive marketing arguments. The white papers combination of educative information and marketing makes it a very powerful content marketing tool.

A well-written whitepaper has the ability to:

a) Create credibility for a company and its products.

b) Enable internal sponsors sensitize their audiences and grow support.

c) Express points of view, create new markets and influence decision-making processes.

d) Reach consumers out of the normal sales chain and convey company messages devoid of distortion.

How to create a white paper:

Identify the problems

Write an introduction of the problems in question, expounding on each to give the reader a general description of each issue and its magnitude. Research on problems from blog posts and other interactive consumer forums and do in-depth analysis on them to obtain proper understanding.

Formulate solutions

Write an introduction containing the solutions you would like to describe in depth in the following sections. Relate them to the problems they attend to, to enhance the flow of the paper. Solutions can be obtained from your own creativity, suggestions from consumer interaction forums or brainstorming sessions from the members of the marketing team.

Conclusion

This section's purpose is to summarize the problem and solution sections, and to introduce the brochure section, assuring the reader that the solutions given are fully implementable.

Brochure section

Give an outline of the business and provide information about the benefits of the product to the consumer as well as provide an avenue through which the reader can contact you for additional information about the product/service.

Write the paper's introduction

This task is left for last because the writer needs to write an introduction that preempts the paper's content, and convinces the reader to read the rest of the paper after reading the first few lines. This task thus requires the author to have in depth knowledge of the paper's content. The introduction is a teaser that sums the paper's contents in less than 500 words.

21. Wiki Pages

Wikis are collaborative websites and pages that allow users to create forums from which numerous members can interact and share information. It primarily requires an individual to create and title the wiki, giving a clear description of the wiki's content. The individual then notifies the people he is interested in sharing it and sets the user privileges of each member - that is, whether the user can view or alter the information provided in the wiki, in whole or in-part, or even add their own pages.

Members of a team require collaborating on project intricacies irrespective of distance. Google Docs provides an avenue for such use. They offer such convenience for free and content is accessible as well as alterable from anywhere on the globe. They require a user to sign up for a free Google account in order to post documents, presentations and spreadsheet documents online and share them with the persons of interest. The user gets the options of assigning interactive protocol for other users of his content thus anyone wishing to do more than just view the content requires authorization from him.

PBWiki has similar wiki functionality and has a package for educators who get an unlimited numbers of users and a 10MB wiki for free; as opposed to the free wiki website that is available for a maximum of three users. The user controls member interaction by categorizing the users as Reader, Writer, Editor or Administrator.

22. QR Codes

Pointing a camera at the image should deliver instant messages, web content, or any other beamed content directly to your smart phone or computer. The most important consideration is that shared information should be standard and offer fast mobile access.

To get started in creating your own QR Codes:

a) Find a QR Code Generator. *Kaywa* is among the most popular simple non-commercial services for creating a quick

QR code. *QR stuff* and *Maestro* are other options offering specific future-sets or a different approach.

b) Add Your Content

c) Create click buttons to select the desired code type. Select the code size knowing bigger sizes offer better options. The 'generate' button facilitates the toggling of size from the same menu.

d) Share It. To add the code, share its permalink, save it into a file or embed it into your blog then print off flyers or business cards.

23. Short & Sweet: SMS & Tweets

Search for the best and latest content to deliver to your customers. These may include a Facebook giveaway, an event or VIP opportunities. Additional benefits may feature accolades from colleagues. Incorporating relevant quotes from Google search, favorite authors, or popular leaders would thrill the viewers as long as the tweeting is done sparingly. Tweeting quotes can also be obtained from blog posts like Technorati. It is essential to ensure you read the blog posts you are tweeting.

Send as many transactional messages as possible and conduct in-store SMS campaigns for a wider market. Retailers might as well consider delivering instant coupons that outline more detailed product information. Focus should be on tweeting relevant information otherwise it would be rendered useless.

24. Apps (Mobile, Facebook)

You can become visible to mobile or desktop users through generic web searches or apps. By providing an app you allow direct access to your company and product offerings, entertain your customers through games or increase brand awareness. Customers can also interact with you directly.

Tools to use to create a mobile app:

MyAppBuilder

Using MyAppBuilder, you can create two Android or iPhone apps at $29 per month. You must provide your desired content to the pros, who will handle the nitty-gritty.

AppMakr

You can also easily create your personal iPhone app through AppMakr. Through this browser-based platform, you can produce several approaches for your application by utilizing social networking feeds and current content. It comprises features like push notifications, custom CSS and location-aware GeoRSS. You can use the tool for free although you can enjoy advanced features through a monthly subscription fee of $79. It's compatible with Android, Windows and iOS operating systems.

25. Widgets and badges

Widgets and badges placed on the website help users identify related products, show your affiliation to certain brands, add aesthetic value to your website and redirect traffic to other sites or pages on your website. For example for blogs you can post your blog badges or widget on blog directories with a high number of users such as *MyBlogLog* and *BlogCatalog*. It enables you to view the avatars of people that viewed your blog on your widget therefore enabling follow up options for conversations. MyBlogLog gives statistical data pertaining to your blogs traffic, thus you can use that as a marketing performance check and estimation tool for advertisement campaigns.

Most micro blogging suites allow their users to post links from other websites to allow them direct traffic to their blogs or other web pages. Therefore, you can use the blogging sites as platforms to get the word about your business out there and possibly attract new clients on a more personal and interactive level.

26. Templates (Wordpress, Tumblr)

If you are skilled in HTML and CSS, you can construct your own custom theme that will include your credentials and therefore link to your site. All the *WordPress Themes* can be found at '/wp-contents/templates/defaults' and all the *Tumblr Themes* are in the Tumblr's Theme Garden.

27. Online Advertisements

Online advertisements enables information posted by the marketers to appear on the consumer's visited sites, thus the consumer will be more informed and traffic flow for the company's website will increase, as the consumer will click on pieces that interest them.

Facebook: An example of this includes advertisements posted on social sites such as Facebook. Facebook offers marketers the option to increase consumer awareness of their products through the 'like' option on the social site.

Mobile: The key principle behind mobile advertising is to enhance company accessibility without being intrusive to the consumer. Advertisements thus have to be made short and direct but keeping them appealing. The fact that the consumer receives them on their mobile phone makes it more personal and enhances the company website's click through rate. Since alternative tabs are not as viable on mobile phones as they are on computers, advertiser need to strive to ensure that the target audience does not feel interrupted or negatively affected by the advertisement when they click on it. This can be done by ensuring that the advertisement is highly relevant to the platform it is displayed on.

LinkedIn: this is an online social site that provides a platform for professional individuals to network in reference to their previous contacts made. It is used to boost resumes and illustrate work history and expertise. Due to its high user number it is a platform that advertisers exploit to try increase their consumer base. It has 175 million users worldwide and advertisers require to profile the users to enable them provide relevant adverts to this class of individuals.

YouTube: since the acquisition of YouTube by Google, it has been made possible to cash in on the viral status of videos online. With the use of banner advertisements on pages that experience a high volume of views, the company was able to maximize ad visibility while encouraging users to post videos to maintain volume of individuals watching.

Twitter: Sponsored tweets and social media posts create large traffics for most advertisers. They connect users with celebrities at a personal level. They also connect companies with celebrities and other social sites with high follower counts, increasing their advertising audience.

3
CONTENT PLANNING

Content planning entails determining how and when content is developed, published, distributed and marketed. It is simply a strategy that helps content managers to develop content and to distribute it within a specific timeframe and for the right audience. The content plan takes into consideration *who, what, how, where ana when* in deciding the type of information to create and put out there.

Some of the benefits of content planning are:

a) It offers a clear picture of the content format

b) It helps to identify the persona of the people who receive this content

c) Marketers are able to determine the needs of their target market before creating or distributing content

d) It provides a guideline for key milestones to be attained in your content development strategy

The 6 Ws: Why, What, Who, Where, When And How

The framework for content development takes into consideration:

The Why: For example, why are you creating this content? Why do you need to target a specific target audience? Why should you use a certain content format at any given time?

The What: What do you want to convey with your content? What objectives do you want to accomplish with this content?

The Who: Who is your target audience? What are their characteristics and their needs? Who are they following, talking and engaging with?

The Where: Where will you distribute your content to ensure it is visible to your target audience? Where does this audience hang out so you can reach out to them?

The When: When should you accomplish certain milestones in your content development strategy? After how long will you see results for your content strategy?

The How: How will you develop, distribute and market the content? How will you reach out to your audience and engage them? How will you measure, track and analyze results?

Here is an example of how you can develop a content plan for a blog:

Define your audience: Determining your buyer persona will help you understand the type of information they are looking for before they can engage with you. Buyer personas are simply the top attributes of your target audience. Keep it simple, identify their characteristics and what they are likely to be looking for to meet their needs.

Schedule: Determine the key deliverables that you need to accomplish in the development and distribution of content. Set a time frame for creating certain content for example videos, white papers, ebooks, and blog posts.

Content Type: What type of content will you deliver to your audience? You need to consider the type of content your audience is most engaged with. In addition to textual content, your audience may also be engaged with videos, professional presentations, podcasts and webinars; or any other type mentioned in the previous chapter.

Calls-to-Action: How will you reach out to your target audience and start to engage them? You can use various calls-to-action such as Facebook competitions and promotions, asking them to download an ebook, or to subscribe to a newsletter or webinar.

Create An Editorial Plan

An editorial plan is a method of planning and managing the development of content. This plan not only gets you organized in your content strategy, it also ensures that you remain consistent with the content you develop. Consistency counts when producing high quality content that will reflect well on your brand.

If you are working with others in the creation of content, an editorial plan allows you to effectively organize the team in terms of research, content development, distribution and marketing. It also shows who is supposed to do what, when and how while at the same time determining the type of content to be created.

In creating an editorial plan, it is best to determine what you want to include in the schedule and what should be excluded. For example, the plan should feature milestones geared towards the constant publication of content. It should also include a strategy for synchronizing content with product launches and marketing efforts.

In addition to this, the editorial plan should take into consideration important dates that determine the type of content to be created. For example mother's day, Christmas day, product campaigns just to mention a few.

An editorial plan should at least contain the content name, the type of content and the source, where it will be distributed, when it will be published and the deadline for content development.

Another important element of the editorial calendar is the metadata. These snippets of information allow you to track the milestones you are working on. The tags you use can be as diverse as is necessary for your tracking. You can include tags related to your target audience, product campaign cycles, the type of content, the publication date and others. The metadata allows you to keep track of your progress while at the same time showing you where you are presently with you content strategy.

The content format is essential. To ensure that you maintain consistency and keep the content relevant to your overall goals, incorporate a *style guide* into your editorial plan. The content style guide can also develop into a social media policy that shows how social media responses and messages should be conveyed. Consistency in your content will ensure that you are not sending different messages about your brand. In the style guide, indicate what the tone of your content will be. Of course, this will depend on your target audience. You also need to consider what you would like to convey through your content. A younger audience may need a friendly and conversational tone when it comes to content marketing. On the other hand, if your content speaks to professional groups, the tone may be informational and straight to the point.

Identify Your Audience And Find Where They Like To Hangout

Before developing content of any type, you want to determine whom you are creating this content for. This entails determining the buyer or customer persona. There are different layers or strata of customers that you are can target. Stratifying you audience starts with using any immediate information you may have about them. This may include their occupation, industry, age, and gender.

Next, personalize the individuals in each of the customer strata. Personalizing entails digging deep into their attributes; what they like, how they spend and what they spend on, their social media engagement, the things they discuss online, the concerns and needs they air, and the comments they make about certain products, services and brands. This will help you to tailor your message in a way the audience can relate to.

Some questions to ask when identifying your audience are:

What type of readers or viewers am I looking for?

Should they fall within a certain category in terms of profession, age, location, gender or interest?

What are the personality attributes of my audience?

What are their needs, desires and passions?

What can I offer to this audience that they will find valuable?

Who is my preferred customer and what do they like and dislike?

After identifying and determining your ideal audience, the next step is finding out where they are. What type of forums and social platforms do they spend their time? Many studies show that a large majority of online consumers are spending much of their time on social networking sites. The average users may spend just half an hour on these platforms, but many users spend hours every week.

Social media should be part of your content planning strategy. Take time to carefully look at major social networks such as Facebook, Twitter, LinkedIn, Pinterest, Google+ and YouTube to find your defined audience. See what they are talking about, what and who they are following and any concerns they may be airing.

As you seek to find where your target audience spends their time, ask yourself this: Where does my key market group network read the news, conduct research, connect with friends and seeks entertainment? While the main social networks are important, consider focusing on Facebook especially for business-to-customer content distribution and LinkedIn for business-to-business content marketing and distribution. These two platforms host the largest number of social network users and it is easier to identify users according to basic demographical information. Video sharing platforms are also attracting a large number of users and they are lucrative places to find your target audience.

Keep Yourself In The Loop On The Latest Trends & Hot Topics

Keeping up with the trending topics in a given industry allow you to stay abreast with what your audience is following and what is interesting to them at any given time. The top trends and hot topics can also serve as sources of blog content.

Blogs are a great place to see what others are saying about a certain topic through their comments. These comments can help you understand what your potential audience reads, what they are interested in and what their needs are. You can subscribe to the RSS feeds of blogs that are pertinent to your niche. *Technocrati* is a service that lets you find high-ranking blogs in any field. You can do this by using relevant keywords to follow blogs that disseminate trending news in your industry.

Social media sites such as Twitter also offer the opportunity to find thought leaders in your industry. You can also use Twitter to find influential people in a specific niche and to start following them and subsequently actively engage them. This enables you to further identify those who are following the influencers and the conversations they are having.

LinkedIn is one of the best ways to link up with industry professionals and key contacts. Through LinkedIn groups, you can start identifying potential audiences that you can reach out to. The people who interact with on this platform can be a source of trending industry information and updates.

Google Alerts lets you define the type of news updates you want to receive in your inbox. By selecting keywords, you will receive real-time news pertaining to the chosen keywords. You can make your keywords and key phrases as specific as you want the results to be.

Online forums dedicated to your niche area can also offer many insights about the trending topics. Online forums and membership sites are typically dominated by influencers, early adopters and mavericks, who are always on the-know about trends and the hot topics in an industry.

These sites can also be a source of content ideas around what people are talking about. You will find both professionals and ordinary contributors on these platforms and their insights can give you ideas on how to meet a certain need to fill a particular gap.

Online news sources and magazines are valuable sources of instant and sometimes in-depth news. Subscribe to several industry magazines and news channels to receive the latest in your niche.

Offline networks are still relevant. Colleagues, trade groups and associations are valuable sources of industry news and trends. Through your offline networks, you may also get insider scoops even before the new hits the online media. Leverage these traditional networks to stay on top of the goings-on in your industry.

Host Surveys & Epolls

As part of your content planning, surveys and online polls are cost effects methods of gaining insights about your target audience. You can easily conduct a poll around any areas that are related to your overall content development, distribution and marketing goals. With these results, you will be in a position to customize your content in a way that speaks to your audience, thereby eliciting greater engagement.

You can use numerous free or premium tools to conduct the surveys. Some good ones are Poll Daddy and Survey Monkey. The results of these surveys can also make interesting content for a website or blog and be shared on other social platforms.

A growing trend is the use of online survey tools that can be linked to social media networks such as Twitter and Facebook. These tools, such as Survey Monkey allow you to effectively survey your social media community right from where they are holding their conversations and networking. Your social media followers are a great group to survey because they have been following your brand and are likely to have valuable and relevant insights.

As you plan to conduct your online survey, be sure to narrow down the groups that you really want to target with your content. This will give you a true picture of what to expect, what to include in your content and how to approach the overall content strategy. Also, keep the surveys short to ensure that your target audience completes it and so you to have comprehensive results.

Conduct A Competitive Analysis

Analyzing your competitor's content strategy will help you to determine how to position your own content. You can start by looking through your competitor's website to see where they have located their content and the type of content they are developing. Does your competition have a single blog or more? What type of content they have on their About Us Page? How have they organized their content in terms of navigation?

You also want to see **the type of content they publish** the most; is it blog posts, ebooks, white papers, videos, audios or articles? How many ebooks have they published? How many blog posts, videos, and whitepapers do they have? Answers to these questions will give you an idea on how your own content publishing efforts stack up to those of your competitors.

In the same vein, identify **how often they publish** their content. Do they do it once a week, once a day? How often do they develop large content such as ebooks or a webinar? This will tell you the competitor's level of activity with regard to content creation.

Finally, determine the type of topics your competition covers in their content so you can leverage any points of advantage they are not leveraging themselves. Use free crawling services such as *Xenu Link Sleuth* to make your content analysis easier.

Next, analyze **the quality of your competitors' content**. Some questions to factor in are: Is their content authoritative and reliable? Is it professionally written in terms of flow, spelling and grammar? Is the content detailed or shallow? How helpful is it for the target audience? Is there just one person creating the content or are there other contributors?

After determining the level of quality, the next step is to look at **how they have linked their content with social media**. Are social media buttons on their blogs and websites to allow users to share the content? It is important to track your competitor's social media engagement so, look around for the major social networks such as *Facebook, Twitter, Pinterest, Google+, YouTube and LinkedIn*. Look at how your competition is engaging on these platforms in terms of the number of followers, subscribers, and repins. What kind of messages and content do they distribute in these social networks? Are they actively involved with their social community?

Research The Keywords That Your Audience Is Likely To Use

How is your target audience likely to search for your content? It is one thing to create content and it is quite another to have it in front of your target audience. This means that you need to research the keywords and phrases your audience is likely to use when searching for you. You will then incorporate these keywords into your search engine optimization strategy to make your content searchable.

In addition to using the keywords in your content, you can use these keywords in your social media engagements. Using these keywords, you can find people to follow and have conversations with. Make use of hashtags related to your keywords to see the trending topics in any given area and to participate in the conversation. Other tools to use are *Twellow* that allows you to look up for businesses with which you can start engaging. *Google External Keyword Tool* will provide a list of keywords and the variations that your prospects are likely to use to find you.

Find The Influencers

Engaging influencers can help you generate buzz around your content once your publish it. Influencers are also valuable sources of information about industry trends, hot topics and developing news. These include reporters, mavens, committed social media users, industry thought leaders, bloggers and marketers. After identifying the influencers, the next step is to determine what motivates them to spread and share information with their network.

Determine the attributes of your targeted influencers, where they spend their time and what their interests are. What language do they speak to reach out to their own social community and how do they distribute their messages in their social conversations.

Look at blogs in your niche to find out who writes them and what they are writing about. This can offer you an opportunity or guest blogging in high ranking and influential blogs where you can attracts your target audience and engage them. The influential bloggers already have an advantage as they have an attentive audience to whom they can introduce your content.

The keywords you researched on previously can also help in identifying influencers. Make use of *Google Insights* for Search to help you determine long tails keywords that will help you generate specific results in terms of finding influential businesses and individuals.

Listening tools have become increasingly important in keeping track of what people in your industry are saying about you or your brand. This will not only keep you up to date with the latest trends but will also show you the influencers you should be interacting with in your field. Some useful listening tools include *Tweetdeck, Social mention, Google Alerts, Open Facebook search, LinkedIn and Google Groups*. By using these listening tools, you can spot the people who are actively engaged in your niche through posting tweets and Facebook messages, creating news article as well as blog posts.

Klout is an indispensible tool when it comes to looking for influencers around social media platforms. Klout is a tool that ranks social media and web users based on their level of activity and the impact that their messages have on followers. If there is anyone in your niche with a high Klout, you want to follow them, create rapport and start to actively engage them. By sharing their content with your social community, they too will be inclined to share yours with their network.

Other useful tools are *Flowtown*, which offers in depth information about influencers in your niche including their emails and access to their social profiles. Use *Twitalyzer* to identify where your influencers are geographically, their online activities and their interests.

Be helpful to your influencers, for example through guest blogging, commenting on their blog posts, retweeting their messages and hashtags and sharing links to their content. It is best if you have a blog already that generates high quality content before engaging with your targeted influencers first. It is also helpful to be actively involved in social media for a period of time before reaching out to the influencers.

4

CONTENT CREATION AND
CONTENT CURATION

Website content creators and publishers have been divided over the pros and cons of curation. Content aggregation – information gathering - (seen on sites such as *Google News*) has existed for some time, however the editorial curation – information categorizing - is a new term. It involves human organizing and filtering as well as discovery, collection, and presentation of digital content focusing on specific subject matters. It then furnishes readers with this information in a mash-up format. The constant flow of information makes it hard for people to gain important tidbits and curated content allows them to find the most important news or information. Through curation, you can meet and connect with other people. People will like you if you share and contribute in non self-promoting ways.

The Difference Between A Content Creator And A Content Curator

Content creators identify their audiences and create authentic and significant content. The content undergoes absorption, appreciation, sharing and re-sharing. Thus, it drives consumers of your content to you.

In contrast, content curators scour the Web to discover and deliver the most vital content. A thoughtful curator identifies the relevancy of their content and the perfect sharing context.

There are some major rules that determine the success of a content curator. Content curation can flop due to certain factors. Examples include failure to give credit or link to the source, utilization of automated curation (automated curation can undermine quality thus human influence is important in content aggregation) and prioritizing quantity (quality of the content should always be foremost as compared to the quantity).

95% of Online Marketers had curated content in the past six months. Curators must mix curation with new content as they are both vital for SEO success. Exercise creativity in your curative works and make your blog more interesting by adding graphical material and videos.

11 Tools For Curation

1. Google News

This news service provider collects and puts together trending and relative content sourced from blogs, newspapers, organizations and online magazines from all over the world on the web and presents it to the viewer in record time.

2. Google Reader

This is a news feed reader that allows users to organize and compile relevant feeds and time-index them enabling users to keep track of the articles they have read.

3. Alltops

This website's aim is to provide a solution to the thirst for current and trending information. It achieves this by compiling the headlines from blogs and sites about a particular topic and then categorizes the compilations under one web page for user friendliness. Five most recent headlines, together with their headlines, are then posted on these pages.

Alltop tools:

Widgets: You can post a widget on a particular topic on your blog. The widget will display the five most recent headlines on the topic thus giving your blog an updated look.

RSS feeds: Alltop's RSS links can be accessed through your browser's navigation area. You can also build your own widget from the RSS feeds or obtain the RSS feed of an individual's MyAlltop page by grabbing the RSS feed of that page.

4. Popurls

Popurls works by compiling the most popular topics from websites and feeds and presenting them on a dashboard where the user is able to view them by topic and feed time. The user is empowered to view everything from all sites in one place and have the convenience of just clicking a link to view the whole story. Popurls combines RSS feeds and news Reader properties in a single application and allows the user to modify the application to best meet his preferences.

5. Topsy

This engine functions by importing links from Google+ and Twitter to determine popular content and enables you to sort out through the feeds, according to time frames, subject, content type and relevance. It is however not possible to filter through feeds from both Twitter and Google+ at the same time. Advanced search options enable the user to:

a)   Track the popularity of certain keywords in the recent past.

b)   Seek out popular images related to search parameters.

c)   Identify reliable sources for information relating to certain keywords.

d)   Share your search results.

6. SocialMention

It sources information from 80 top popular social sites and search engines worldwide and streams it to users. Apart from search facilities this site offers tools that enable you to follow what people are saying about a particular subject. It also allows you to receive alerts every time new information pertaining to your keywords is obtained and provides a widget to post on your blog or site.

7. Flipboard

This is an interactive iPad application that monitors the tweets and Facebook posts you post to friends, compiles them and displays them as a digital interactive magazine. All you need to do is subscribe to your posts.

8. Scoop.It

It is a curation platform with a magazine like format that allows users to gather information online and post on it. Users can either manually add content on the site or allow the site's automated search engine post related content from various sites. Scoop.It can also be used as a platform for sharing original works or pursuing of business related marketing activities. It comes in three plans: free, expert and business plans. The free edition is limited in terms of capability but still meets the basic curating needs.

9. Storify

This site, Storify.com, allows the user to search out content and conduct research on the web and post it on its website. The user then gives the story a title and introduction. All the user needs to do is drag the selected curated content and drop it on the Storify window. This however requires one to be logged in to Storify. The user can add content and images and other real-time information such as tweets.

10. CurationSoft

It allows searching content by keyword from several content sources such as Twitter, Flickr, YouTube, Google News and blogs. It only includes properly licensed content.

11. Technorati

After searching through the comprehensive list of blogs on Technorati you can check the related tags as they can also lead to more comprehensive key phrases.

12. Google+ Search

The Google+ Your World personalization feature produces search results from Google+. You can view previously unseen content by connecting with new people on Google+. This is due to the incorporation of shared and recommended sites from your Google+ friends by Search Plus Your World. By clicking on any autosuggested name, your friends' Google+ profiles and additional information will appear. Also, you can scour their Google+ profiles directly for content.

Rules for Content Engagement And Results

Provide Solutions

It is a good idea to show how your product works, not just to say it. This is possible through well-worded case studies or success stories. Case studies can be created through focusing on problems that face customers, how your product solved it and the results.

Educate

Evergreen and ever-useful are two words that epitomize good web content. Unlike news stories, evergreen content never becomes stale to readers. The creation of great content involves a lot of work.

Value Provision

When writing online content, you must produce unique content. Avoid copying or plagiarizing other websites' contents. The same rule applies to writing content for Search Engines such as, Yahoo, Bing or Google. To gain credibility and interest from the audience, remember to incorporate relevant resources.

Highly Visual

Content relevancy can also accrue through the addition of relevant images. Images add gloss to a text-littered and dry environment. As attention grabbers, they provide sensual space and visual pleasure. Many acclaimed bloggers embed images within their feeds. This transforms the feeds into full feeds.

Form A Series

You should adhere to a single thought train and avoid confusing the readers. This saves you time and enhances the article's relevancy and forthrightness. Creating a series is beneficial to writers with a lot of ideas for one topic. You must segment the ideas to avoid content cluttering. Avoid side issues that are deadwood and transfer them to the idea list. Also, provide a mixture of advance planning and tightly focused subjects.

Be Witty And Conversational

Web writing involves feedback and discussions from the audience on important issues. Create interesting content to successfully market yourself, your services and products. Use humor and write the content like you were trying to convince yourself into engaging your own services.

Inspiration and storytelling

Your first paragraph should capture your readers' interest immediately. Lifeless or dull paragraphs are sure to lower their interest. People come to the web for fast and great information. Your content should also be straightforward. Avoid overindulging in sales pitch as your readers can always seek you out when they need more information.

5
CONTENT OPTIMIZATION

Content optimization is an important aspect of an SEO campaign. It is a continuous process of modifying and organizing the content on your website to boost its appeal, relevance and quality not just for the search engines but also for site users. Content optimization is ideally the strategic use of targeted keywords and phrases within the website copy, to ensure that the content can be found for the relevant search words. Here are some factors to take into consideration when optimizing for the end user and the search engines:

8 Types Of Online Searches

Web users use different types of search engines platforms to find different type of content. Some common searches include:

Social Search: A social search engines takes into consideration the social graph of the web user who queries the search engine. The relevance of the search results is determined by the content of each document and the link arrangement of these documents. The social search results provide greater visibility to content that is created by other users who belong to the social graph. Social searches can be in the form of shared bookmarks, tagged content, images, videos, podcasts, knowledge sharing platforms and web pages that other users have created and shared.

Global Search: Global search entails the use of global platforms to generate less localized searches and web pages. Unlike local searches that generate content specific to a particular geographical location, a global search generates results from all over the web and really, from all parts of the world. Global content optimization would therefore entail the creation of multilingual websites and keyword optimization to ensure accessibility by users from all parts of the world. In optimizing content for a global audience, a webmaster considers the cultural differences of their target audience.

Local Search: Local search involves querying search engines for localized information in a specific geographical location. This type of search is especially important for local businesses looking to gain greater visibility among local customers. Users utilize local searches such as Yelp,

Google+ local to find locations, recommendations for businesses, places to eat, shop and visit.

While global searches are important, local searches are gaining greater significance as more and more businesses gain an online presence. Local search engine optimization entails making your business and website visible to those who have physical proximity to the business.

Product Search: As ecommerce continues to gain popularity among web users, shoppers are using product search platforms to find and compare products. Platforms such as *Nextag* and *Google+ Local* allow user to read reviews and recommendations and compare prices before buying a product. Product searches lets user find products, event tickets, books, sales and promotions, travel plans and even real estate sales.

For merchants, content optimization in product search engine entails selecting and paying for specific areas on the platform where your listing will appear. It may also involve optimizing content for either local or global search according to the target audience.

Photo Search: Searching and sharing images is a prominent activity of web users. Photo search engines allow users to find a wide range of images. Users can sort images by color, JPG, PNG, BMP and GIF formats. *Google Image Search* is the most common photo search engine. Others include *Flickr Images* that allows access to photos with copyrights and others that are governed by the Creative Common License allowing web users to utilize the images with some reserved rights. On the part of a webmaster, image optimization will require the proper use of tags and Alt text that contain descriptive keywords for the images.

Video Search: more and more web users are accessing video content through their mobile devices as well as from their web browsers. Video search offers users access to videos with content such as music, podcasts, instructional material, promotional advertisements, among others. Video search engines such as *YouTube Search* analyze the web to find video content with the relevant tags and display them on the search engine results page. To optimize video content to make it visible at the search engines, it is important to include relevant tags, keywords and key phrases related to the video content.

Event Search: Event search engines such as *SocialVent* allow web users to search and find events globally. The search results are displayed on *Google Maps* allowing the user to know the exact location of the event. Users can search events by location, date, and categories such as art, food, business, fashion, music and many more. By clicking on the event location on Google Map for example, the user will be able to see more details of the event including exact address, the time and date, admission costs and any relevant information pertaining to the event.

Reviews Search: Consumers are becoming fussier about the brand they will buy from and the type of product or service they are willing to pay for. Review sites are an integral part of the decision making process for many consumers today. People are resorting to reviews search engines to find relevant review and forum sites where other users offer their recommendations and opinions about a product, service or brand.

Review search engines such as *TravelAdvisor* enable consumers to access travel related information such as hotel quality or restaurants services. Other third party review searches that you can ask customers to post reviews about your product, service or brand are *Yahoo!*, *InsiderPages*, and *City Search*.

Short Vs. Long

Often marketers wonder whether they should be creating long articles and video or shorter ones. There is a general agreement that there isn't just one way to go about this; you can create a mix of both long and short articles depending on various factors such as the topic at hand or the message you intend to put across to your audience. Sometimes, shorter articles are better at conveying certain messages while longer ones will better serve in-depth topics.

The advantage of short content is that you can be entertaining and informative at the same time. Readers may be in a better position to stick around and read what you have to say. Also, while you cannot cover all sides of a topic in one short article, you can spread out the topic in several short articles over a period of time. Seth Godin, for example has mastered the art of creating short, thought provoking posts that are offered every day.

Learning to convey a message in short content can help you to be concise and to the point with the content. This is especially true for blog posts and videos; large majorities of web users are more inclined to engage with content that gets straight to the point than winding posts and videos. Nevertheless, if you are targeting an audience that is likely to be looking for detail for example marketing professionals, you might want to post longer content for your blog posts or create longer podcasts and webinars.

Longer pieces of content allow you to cover all sides of a presentation or a topic at a go. However, it is best to cover a single topic in any one piece of content be it a video, an audio, podcast or blog post. This ensures that the content remains relevant to the user. Another great advantage of longer content is that it encourages readers to comment and discuss about the message in the piece of content. While short content can still be commented on and discussed, longer content has greater potential for triggering this kind of user interaction and dialogue.

On a similar note, it is not always true that shorter video content will go viral as opposed to longer ones. Admittedly, at the peak of *YouTube* video virility, shorter videos (those that lasted less than 10 minutes) were more popular within the video viewing community. However because YouTube has increased the video limit from 10 to 15 minutes, video content can still be longer and go viral. Platforms such as *VeVo* have also made it possible to upload longer video content.

The bottom line is that quality really matters more than the length of the content. In a video, for example, viewers are likely to be hooked by the first 15 seconds of the content, regardless of whether the video is long or short. This also applies to blog posts; creating interesting and informative content is likelier to engage readers regardless of length.

Link Building

Link building is an essential element of search engine optimization. Through links, search engine robots are able to determine how popular a website and pages on a site are depending on the quality of the links. Other metrics that search engines consider in determining the quality of links are trust and authority. Trustworthy and authoritative links typically link to other trustworthy and authoritative links.

Internal Linking: Many webmasters overlook internal links as a link building strategy, yet it is one of the most effective. Internal link building entails linking one page in a website to another in the same website or domain. Internal links enable users to easily move from one page on a website to the next. Importantly, they boost the website or blog ranking in search engines as the link authority is spread out across the website.

If there is a page on your website that is particularly important, it is essential that you optimize it for the search engines. For the search engines to rank this important page, it will analyze how many other pages are pointing to this page that you seek to optimize. For example, it better to link your blog to the main homepage of a website in addition to the 'About Us' pages. This will allow search engines to rank the blog pages as one of the most valuable on your website.

To effectively link internally, you need to consider how you have already linked some of your pages and whether this approach is effective. One way to optimize the internal links is to pay attention to the topics you often create content around. Then, create another page dedicated to this type of content. Each post will then link to this dedicated page. Additionally, take into consideration where the dedicated page is located on the website's navigation. Determine whether it is suitable to link it to the homepage or product page, depending on your type of business.

Link Baiting: Link baiting simply means the creation and distribution of great content aimed at generating backlinks from other platforms such as blogs and websites. Marketers should invest time and resources on this link building strategy.

<u>What type of content will attract valuable backlinks?</u>

How-To-Guides and instructional content that show people how-to so effectively do something: It is a good idea to link to other authoritative and relevant sites to improve the credibility of your instructional video. It is also important to highlight your credentials or expertise within the content.

Viral content: If you host the content on an independent site, link this domain back to the primary company site. At the end of the viral campaign, create a 301 link that redirects the content back to the main website.

Multi-media: Videos, images, podcasts and webcasts that you create can be linked back to your site, thereby boosting your site's visibility at the search engines.

Top ten lists, polls and surveys: Top ten lists make for great content that is easily linkable back to your site. You can create a top ten list on just about anything that pertains to your niche. Other websites and bloggers are also likely to link back to polls and surveys you conducted and that are relevant to their own content or audience.

SlideShare: It is feasible to leverage third party content sharing platforms such as SlideShare to distribute content that is directly linkable to your main site. For example for SlideShare, you can create a straightforward but professional powerpoint presentation or product reviews. Other web users who access this content and find it helpful will link back to your site just be sure to include your site URL in all your presentations. Also, include images and optimize them with relevant keyword rich descriptions. Additionally, include a call-to-action to prompt users to click back to your site.

Squidoo: is also another content sharing site that adds back links to your site. For example, the RSS feed option allows you to create an RSS feed for your blog and any other content property you may have. Then you can paste the link to your RSS feed in your Squidoo lens to create authoritative backlinks.

Keyword Density

Keyword density is the percentage of the number of keywords in relation to the total number of words in an article. As seen above, the use of keywords is an important part of your search engine optimization strategy. However, keywords need to be used effectively for search engines to adequately crawl your content and rank it.

The recommended keyword density is 1% to 3%. To determine the keyword density, you need to know the total number of words in an article and the number of times you have used the keyword or key phrase. For example, a 500-word article with keywords used 5 times will have a keyword density of 1%.

How do you go about achieving the right keyword density and effectively optimizing content for the search engines? First, be sure to use the keyword or key phrase in the post **title** or on the page where the post appears. The title should of course be related to the content and should be compelling. It is important that the keywords appear naturally within the title.

In the content, use the keyword **in the first paragraph** and preferably in the first sentence of this first paragraph. Similarly, use the keyword **in the last paragraph**. Applying the keywords in this way allows the search engine to determine what the article is about. The keywords must appear naturally within the main content as well.

Use the keyword **in the description** Meta tag as well as in the keyword Meta tag. The description Meta tag informs the search engines what the content, site or page entails. The description tag, which appears just after the main title of a page or a post, should ideally be 155 characters long. This the brief piece of information that appear just below the title in the search engine results page.

To enable the search engines to understand the content on your website pages, it is important to create a good description. The description should offer brief and accurate insights about the page. Google search robots will replace an inaccurate description with its own description to tell web users what the content is about. Creating your own description is better than leaving it to Google. Remember to use the secondary keyword at least once in the description meta tag.

Page Optimization

SEO techniques tend to be classified as on-page and off-page optimization. The most common form of off-page optimization is external link building. On-page optimization entails organically optimizing content on website pages by taking into consideration factors such as title tags, meta tags, keywords and URL. Some tips for page optimization are:

URL Optimization: It appears that shorter URLs have a better performance on the search engine results page when compared to longer ones. Shorter links are also easily shared, copied and linked to other sites by users across the web.

Keywords: Concerning the keywords, it is best to use a primary keyword on your page URL. Although this is not one of the major ranking factors, it will still play a significant role on page optimization. For example you can optimize the page using a keyword as such: example.com/keyword instead of example.com/folder/subfolder/keyword. The aim here is to bring the keyword as close to the URL as possible. Additionally, when optimizing the page URL, it is recommended to use hyphens in separating keywords within the URL. However, it is best not to use hyphens to separate words in the root domain names. Hyphen separation performs better in sub domains. For example, redmarketing.com (root domain) is more preferable to red-marketing.com.

Title optimization: The page title tag is one of the most crucial elements in web optimization. It is important that the title tag is kept brief but it should offer adequate description about the page content to site visitors. The page title is the first element that appears on the search engine results pages. Ensure that the site name or your business name appears in the title of the page. This is especially applicable if you anticipate that potential site visitor may look for you using a business name. Placing this name at the title tag will allow users to see it at the search results page. Place primary keywords in the title tag if you are looking to rank highly for these keywords. It is important to create compelling titles that are naturally readable by humans and by the search engines as well.

Body Tags: Within the page body, it is best to consider factors such as keyword density. You might want to repeat a keyword 2 to 3 times in shorter pages and about 4 to 6 times for longer pages. Adding too many keywords than is necessary will amount to keyword stuffing and this will stifle your page ranking at the search engine pages.

In addition, content optimization through keyword variation is recommendable. While this might not solely boost your page rankings, it will work hand in hand with other techniques such as proper keyword density usage. Use one or two versions of the keyword or key phrases to allow the page to be searchable by more than one keyword or key phrase.

Another consideration is the **H1 tag**. A good technique is to use the H1 tag as the page headline. It is also advisable to include relevant keywords and key phrases in the H1 tag. Admittedly, H2, H3, H4 tags etc, do not appear to have a significant effect on page optimization.

The Alt description has a strong potential for page optimization. It is advisable to use images and representations within keyword targeted and high-importance pages such as the homepage or the product page. Include the keyword or phrase in the Alt attribute of the image tag. Additionally, use target keyword or phrase as the image file on the page where the image appears.

Images can attract significant traffic to a website, when adequately optimized. The Alt attribute is a description of the image tag and serves as an alternative text in the event that a browser does not display an image. An effective alt text should be brief to keep the browser from splitting up the text. The alt text is not meant to fully describe the image but to contextualize the image.

The alt tag should also be clear as much as it is brief. Note, that some users will only see the alt text and not the images; a text that is too brief may not clearly convey the content of the image. For example, 'a top' is a good description, 'a green top' is even better, while 'a green top with long sleeves that would not look too good on a short person' is too much of an alt text.

Provide context for your image instead of describing in length. This will allow you to keep the alt tag brief and clear. Additionally, your alt text should not seek to explain the technical aspects of your site. Most importantly, the alt tags should be optimized for the search engines, for example by including the relevant keywords.

An element that is often overlooked is **the use of bold and emphasized fonts for keywords**. It recommended making the keyword bold at least once within the page body. Italicized fonts seem to have greater weight in terms of page rakings; italicize the target keywords at least once within the page content.

HTML Tags: Optimizing HTML tags allows you to highlight some important elements in your page. One important HTML tag element is the title. It is important that the first word in the title be the keyword or key phrase as this is likely to boost the page rankings. The further away the keyword moves in the title, the lesser its ranking potential.

Although **Meta descriptions** are not as important to the major search engines, this area still influences the bolding effect that appears in the visual snippet on the search engine results page. The proper formatting of the Meta description can help to enhance click through rates and may as such boost traffic from the page's ranking. Ensure that your site Meta robots do not prohibit page access by the search engines.

If you have a large website, applying a **canonical URL tag** is important. The canonical URL is the domain you want to appear in search results pages and the one that web users will access to find your site and pages. Applying the canonical URL ensures that duplicate sites and pages are not created as this may disallow the search engines from ranking your site adequately.

Internal Link Optimization: When optimizing internal links on a page, it is suggested that the competitive keyword be placed higher on the page. This ensures that from the homepage, users can get to a specific page in just a few clicks.

It is beneficial to link other site pages to pages that are more links to it. This will go a long way in boosting the page rankings of the other less linked-to pages. Additionally, it is valuable to include internal link within the page content or the body of an article instead of placing it as a permanent or fixed navigation. If you choose to apply an internal link in the permanent navigation, it is better to place it right at the top of the content to optimize the page.

Translation

While some web users may read your content in English, it is important to consider the global audience that may prefer to interact with your content in their own language. Optimizing your content and website through translation not only caters for your global audience but it also gives you a competitive edge.

Audiences who can access a site using their own language are likely to remain loyal to that site as long as it caters to their needs. It might also be easier for your website to have higher search rankings in foreign search engines as the competition is less fierce than it is, say on Google English.

However, translation is more than directly changing words from one language to another. Translation for SEO purposes must apply localization techniques that consider factors such as language and cultural nuances. First, the target keywords you are looking to translate may vary in meaning, usage and importance from one language to another. While the keyword may rank well in American or, it may not perform as well in Australian/British English or in Spanish, for example.

Additionally keyword variations in one language may have just one word or meaning when translated into another language. This complexity in keyword translation calls for dedicated keyword research. You might want to use a native speaker or a SEO/Translation company to ensure that the target keywords in your content are appropriate for your global audience.

Do not just translate; localize your content. This means that you have to understand the cultural nuances of the audience you are targeting. How do they use certain words? How are the web users likely to search for a certain product, brand or service? For example, the British audience may use the term 'toss' while the American audience may use 'throw' to mean the same thing. To appeal to your audience and to tap into their search trends, you would have to configure your content in such a way that considers these seemingly subtle nuances. Localization also entails including names of places in the country you are translating for. For example, if you were looking to translate and localize for New Zealand, you would include the initials 'NZ' in your keywords.

Google Translate is often used for site translation. However, the tool may not be adequate especially if you are translating for SEO purposes. It is suggested that you use a translation and SEO company in your multilingual content optimization strategy.

Real-Time Content

Used properly, hashtags (#), whether in Facebook, Twitter, Pinterest or Google+, can help in distributing your message effectively and in real-time. This allows your content to continuously be visible to your audience. A hashtag also creates and generates a conversation around your content and further allows the topic category to become searchable at the search engines.

Hashtags arrange tweets and posts into groups and organize this content around a specific topic. The string of conversation continues to build up as you and those in your social community continue to post messages and hold conversations around a topic. At the end of it all, you have in fact curated user-generated content around a topic. To optimize your tweets or social network posts, you can add hashtags with relevant keywords to make the content searchable and visible to other users. For example, you may use the #marketing hashtag for a tweet or post pertaining to marketing.

What can you do with the curated content? It can make for an interesting post in your blog or a suitable page in your website. The content can appear as real-time testimonials on your website about your brand or product.

To be effective in your hashtags campaign, it is best to keep the message brief and to the point. Shorter and interesting hashtags are more likely to be shared across social networking platforms. While Twitter allows for up to 140 characters, it is best if a hashtag is about 15 characters long. Even though the hashtag should ideally be short, they should also convey a clear message.

Include Calls-To-Action

Calls-to-action are particularly important in lead generation campaigns and can also help to make your content more visible to your target audience. The message is as important as the technical aspects of including a call-to-action in your web pages.

First, you can draw attention to content for example a downloadable ebook by enlarging the size of the call-to-action button. This will certainly make the sign up page or the download link more visible to site visitors. Alternatively, you may place your call-to-action icon at a prominent location such as at the top of a page. This can attract a higher landing page conversion as site visitors are able to notice the call-to-action and adhere to it.

It is possible to have more than one call-to-action to emphasize the urgency of undertaking a certain action. A secondary call-to-action just as the site visitor is almost at the end of a piece of content can prompt the visitors to undertake the action. For example, a primary call-to-action may be to purchase or freely download an ebook. A secondary call-to-action may direct users to a product page that offer more information about the downloadable ebook.

The call-to-action you include in your pages must demonstrate value if you want site visitors to click through and undertake the action. Web users are looking for offers, that are valuable to them and will meet their needs. Thus, list the benefits of what you are offering and then pick the best benefit. Subsequently, craft this benefit into a short message that will be sure to attract site visitor's attention for example 'Download Free Ebook To Find The 5 Secrets Of ...'.

The call-to-action should convey importance. Show your audience why they should be paying attention to your offering. You can do this by showing that what you are offering is seasonal, it is only beneficial if one takes action now or today, it is special (as in special offers that are limited).

It is an added benefit to make your calls-to-action current, according to trends in your industry. This opens up channels of communication between you and your audience. Through an RSS feed, you can inform your audience about any special offers and newsworthy insights in your field. Then, you can ask them to provide comments and opinions about a trend in your industry, thereby creating and curating content around a certain newsworthy topic.

Have A Catchy Headline

The headline is the first thing that your potential readers see and will have an impact on whether they will go ahead and engage with your content. A headline alone plays a significant role in the prospect conversion process. Creating a catchy headline therefore means that you are conveying value to the prospective readers in exchange for their time.

Headlines can be direct or indirect. They can also be instructional or question based, for example: 'How to Write a Novel' (Instructional) or 'Do You Want To Become a Successful Business Owner?' (Question). Headlines can have call-to-actions or be explanatory, for example: 'Hire a New Team Member Today!' (call-to-action or command headline) or 'Why You Should Hire A New Team Member' (offers an explanation).

Lastly is the testimonial type headline, which can be every effective in drawing attention. This entails using what someone has said about your business or you, as the heading.

The type of headline you choose largely depends on what you wish to convey. Overall, the headline should offer value to the user to prompt him to continue reading. Additionally, the headline must be created for the target audience; this ensures that the audience relates to your content and may be prompted to take action. In addition, ensure that your headline has some elements of uniqueness that will interest the prospective user to read on.

6

CONTENT DISTRIBUTION AND MARKETING AUTOMATISATION

You have created your content and optimized it for your target audience and for the search engines, how do you ensure that this content gets to the hands of this audience? A content marketing and distribution strategy allows you to provide valuable content to consumers through the right channels and with a format that they can easily access. Marketing automation also entails channeling your content in a way that it is always available to your audience, while still maintaining its relevance. There are numerous content marketing and distribution channels to leverage.

Where To Distribute Your Content?

Your Blog

Blogs are an excellent channel for content distribution and automation, due to efficiency of the RSS and the ease of external blog linking. As a marketer, you can use your blog to serve as a reliable source of information to your clients and prospects. Blog posts are dynamic enough to be liked to social networks thereby providing a constant flow and exchange of content. The conversation that your community is having on the social network can make for interesting content for your blog readers. It is also a valuable source for blogging ideas. Install an RSS feed in your blog so that site visitors who subscribe to your feed can receive your blog posts automatically whenever you post them.

A tool such as *Posterous* can be helpful in setting up a simple blog through which you can distribute your content. Like other micro-blogging platforms, it is best to use Posterous with your main blog to share short posts, videos, quotes, links and images through email. Users can post on their blog from anywhere, given that the service is optimized for mobile. You can also link your Posterous account with your other social profiles and blogs.

Post As A Guest Blogger

Posting as a guest blogger can be an effective way of exposing your content to a wider audience beyond your own blog. In creating and distributing content through guest blogging, it is certainly best to develop a good working relationship with the blog owner. You can start by following their blog and sharing these posts across the social network.

Social networking platforms such as Facebook are also suitable grounds for the start of a collaborative relationship. Then, you can contact the blog owner through email for example, and pitch to him about the blogging idea.

For your articles to appear in popular blogs with a high page ranking, your content must be high of quality and relevant to the blog visitors. Good content will hardly have a hard time getting published. Guest blogging platforms such as about.com have their own regulations and requirements for publishing an article. These could be formatting requirements, keyword usage or presentation of the article in terms of content.

Article Submission Sites

Article submission DoFollow sites are among the most popular article marketing and distribution channels for the new marketer. While these sites can be effective for article marketing, success depends on the strategy one takes. One mistake new marketers make is to distribute their articles to as many ezines as possible to leverage the free article submission services.

A better approach is to look for high-ranking directories to submit the articles. Lower ranking ones will not offer your content as much visibility as you would like. It is likely that they will not appear in the search engine results page.

The lower ranking directories will also not contribute significantly to your linking popularity nor will they generate adequate traffic to your site. On the contrary, high-ranking article submission directories and sites will deliver these objectives: link popularity, traffic generation and high page rankings at the search engines.

These sites also have their own requirements before they can publish your articles. The top ranking article submission sites typically have stringent regulations and human editors who ensure that all submitted articles adhere to these guidelines.

Articles should be compelling, informative, unique and grammatically correct. Links within the article are usually not acceptable and may need to be placed down at the author bio area. Keyword density requirements are also something to watch out for when distributing content through article ezines and directories.

Services such *99centarticles.com* can help you create high quality articles that are optimized for the search engines and press releases that you can distribute to professional directories.

Press Releases Sites

Creating and distributing well-written press releases can be beneficial in creating buzz about your business. It can also serve to attract useful traffic to your site while at the same time allowing the media to give you that much-needed coverage.

High-ranking press release sites have strict requirements for publishing. The sites are particularly keen on the format as well as the use of images. It is important to include a brand logo on the press releases you distribute. This will give reporters a quick idea of who you are. Include your name as the contact person, your position as well as your contact details.

Press releases are like pieces of news and as such, they need to be timely. As you develop the release, take a view that will be interesting to you target audience and to your existing market. Some good PR submission sites are: *Prweb, Prnewswire* and *Marketwire.*

LinkedIn Groups

LinkedIn is one of the best professional networking sites that also creates an opportunity for content sharing through professional groups. Users can form or join groups according to their professional interests. LinkedIn groups not only serve as a source of business opportunities but also offer ready audiences for your content.

Simply use the site's search engine to find the appropriate group that relates to your professional interest and niche. You want to demonstrate your expertise within these groups by first participating in the ongoing discussions. See what people are asking and if you think you have an appropriate and comprehensive answer go ahead and provide it.

As you establish your authority as an expert in your group, you will be in a position to point people to your website or to content products such as ebooks, webinars and podcasts as well as blog posts. From here, you can escalate your campaign by converting your prospects into warm leads.

In addition to leveraging LinkedIn Groups in this way, marketers can also make use of the ads program. The Group Statistic feature allows you to really target your audience instead of creating untargeted ads.

By using the Group Statistic feature, you can determine groups that are most active and are thus likely to spend more time on the platform. This feature further helps in determining the location (city) where group users work, their professional position and their niche. These statistics can help you to target your advertising content in a way that will yield positive results for your content marketing campaign.

Another useful way of distributing content through LinkedIn is by linking your blog to your bio on the social network. This allows other users to see your blog posts from your profile every time you post. This can be an effective way of attracting LinkedIn traffic to your site via the blog.

Content marketing on professional networks such as LinkedIn is more effective when you take the time to point users to other useful content other than yours. Therefore, in addition to promoting your content be sure to add value to your followers by sharing content generated by others and may be relevant to your network.

While promoting other people's content may not generate traffic to your site it will keep you visible in your network's feed. This then increases the chance of them seeing and reading your content when you post it.

Finally, ask those who have downloaded your content to leave reviews or comment about it within the group discussion board. Customer recommendations and reviews can add to your credibility and that of your content and can encourage more people to download the content.

Facebook

The Facebook timeline feature offers a snapshot of your most recent activities on the platform. It also highlights the newsfeed system that gives users updated information on your activities in real-time. This can be an effective way of distributing and marketing your content albeit small bits of it.

The remodeled timeline feature allows users to post content that is displayed at the top of the page for seven days. The content (text or image) can be highlighted by placing it in a larger box. This area of the page offers an opportunity for marketing by making use of the available banner space at the top across the page. However, the content you place here should be informative, relevant to other users, and not promotional.

Use the newsfeed feature that is part of the timeline to distribute constant content to your fans. Facebook fans can be loyal and most of them tend to spend a lot of time on the platform. However, things do change fast and to stay relevant, you need to post interesting content regularly.

The messages you post on Facebook are essentially content about your business and products. However, do not dwell solely on your brand and product offering; point your fans to other valuable content. In addition, the new timeline enables you to highlight content according to its importance. This way, you are able to decide how to distribute your content to make it visible to your fans.

PostPost is a tool you can use with your Facebook account to manage content. The tool aggregates the conversations in your Facebook stream into an online newspaper style. You can link this to your blog or other social networks to serve as interesting curated content for your followers and readers. Simply log in to postpost.com with your Facebook login details and the magazine containing your Facebook stream will be set up.

Twitter

Using Twitter for content marketing is one of the most effective channels due to the real-time nature of communication on the platform. However, there is more to sharing content on Twitter than bombarding followers with promotional message. A better approach is to point followers to content that is valuable and interesting. This can be your content as well as other news articles, blogs posts, videos, images and webinars other than your own.

To be successful with social media marketing, users need to see that you are worth following given the resourceful information you provide. By offering valuable information to followers, they are likely to retweet your messages and links thereby assisting you to distribute your content further. Twitter is an interactive social network that requires users to reciprocate actions by other users. As others retweet your content, make it part of your content strategy to retweet great content sent to you by those you are following. This is especially important when originator of the tweet is an influencer.

Make use of Twitter Lists to build relationships that will open up new channels for distributing and marketing your content. Lists cannot only start a conversation with the people you have included in your list. They also expand your pool of resources people that you can point other users to. *Hootsuite* and *Tweetdeck* are effective tools that you can use to automate your tweets. In addition to letting you manage more than one Twitter account, and other social media accounts, these tools allow you to continuously engage with your followers.

Even as you automate your tweets, it is imperative to personalize these messages; you want to truly engage with the people who receive these messages. Relevance and proper timing are important when it comes to using these content automation tools.

Another great tool is *CoTweet*, a social media management tool that lets you organize your social media marketing content across different accounts. In addition to keeping your social marketing campaign organized, CoTweet is useful for businesses that have different people or departments involved in social media content distribution.

Pinterest

For many marketers, a pertinent question when it comes to using Pinterest is whether they can generate inbound links using the site. Pinterest strictly prohibits outright promotion. However, a large majority of its users market their brands through the content they post on the site. Images are the primary type of content on this micro-blogging and social networking platform. The links placed on Pinterest are no-follow and as such, the site may not be an immediate resort in your SEO strategy.

Nevertheless, Pinterest can make your content, primarily images and videos, visible to a large and niche specific audience. Commenting and repining options also allow users to connect with others and build worthwhile relationships with those in your specific niche.

To make the most of Pinterest, distribute high quality images of your products, valuable infographics and short interesting videos that can be re-pinned. While the links you post in Pinterest are no follow, the content can still act as a call-to-action compelling people back to your site. Even if your business is service based, you can post interesting quotes and interesting images and videos you find on other websites.

Use keywords and relevant tags to enable your content to be found easily. Distribute your pins to other social networking sites to attract more interest and traffic to your site. To see the effectiveness of your content distribution on Pinterest, use tools such as *Pinerly*.

Google+

Although Google+ is relatively new compared to other social networks, it offers greater opportunity for connecting with people with whom you share interests. This means that you have a better chance of channeling your content to an audience that is likely to be more receptive to it.

Google+ Sparks is especially beneficial for content marketers as it enables you to easily share the content you receive through your Sparks feed. Google+ Sparks is essentially an alerts feed that appears constantly in your Google+ dashboard. Creating a spark entails choosing the type of news or content that you want to receive. You can then share this content with those in your Google+ Circles.

Google+ users are particularly active in sharing, commenting and distributing content. This offers you an opportunity to create niche specific circles of users who are influential and are effective at sharing content with those in their own circles. Use the *Google+ User Directory* to influencers on the platform. Google+ allows you to create as many circles as you want. The content you receive from those in your various circles can also be shared with your social networks on other platforms.

YouTube

Video viewership is on the rise in most major markets across the globe. Marketers are realizing the potential that video content holds in advertising and marketing a brand and its products. YouTube videos attract millions of views every day and these have served to bring lesser-known brands in front of a wide audience. Instead of posting a one off video on YouTube, make this video sharing platform your long-term content distribution and marketing venue. One-way to do this is to create a channel that you can cost effectively customize to reflect your brand.

You do not have to be a YouTube partner or invest in a branded channel. For example, you can customize your background by using your brand colors. This will add credibility to your brand and to your content compared to using the generic backgrounds on the site.

Make use of playlists that allow you to organize your video content for users to find videos easily. Create playlists that best demonstrate your products and those that have received the most viewership. Remember to optimize your video content by using targeted keywords in the video title.

As you describe your content, start with a complete URL that links to a preferred domain. Provide an adequate description of your video content and use the relevant keywords in the description. This ensures that your videos are searchable within YouTube and on the organic search pages of major search engines.

The Post Bulletin options allow you to create alerts and provide links to the videos that appear on users' homepage. When people subscribe to your channel, they will be alerted about any new content you have created. These bulletins can help in traffic generation for your content.

Vimeo

Vimeo is a video-based social network that allows users (especially artists) to post high quality videos onto the site to showcase their works. The site is very niche specific in that large majorities of users are particularly interested in video and video content. For a small site, it generates significant traffic accounting for 13,000 clips each day.

The major requirement for distributing video content on Vimeo is that you need to have participated in the creating on the video. While this platform is less popular when compared to YouTube, some content marketers may prefer it for various reasons. First, users have adequate control over their content as videos are placed in their accounts. As such, other users have to come to your account to view your videos.

This also means that your videos are not placed against other competing content that also include ads by other brands. Finally, once your video ends, it does not promote similar content, as is the case with YouTube. Another factor that is attracting marketers to Vimeo is that it is less cluttered in terms of content and as such offers greater opportunity and less competition.

Viddler

Viddler is an interactive video-sharing site created specifically for businesses. Users can share existing video files or record new ones using a webcam. The site provides the Person, Business and Partner accounts. The personal one if free but the space for video uploading is limited. Regardless of the account you use, your video content is optimized for mobile phones and mobile devices as well as for desktops.

Users can add tags, include links, threading conversations and real-time comments to their video content. Due to the interactive nature of this platform, it is possible for marketers to hold contests around your brand to attract attention and traffic for you videos. For example, you can host a contest encouraging user-generated videos around a specific topic. Also, Viddler offers widgets to allow users to embed videos in their website or blog.

Tumblr

Tumblr is a micro blogging service that enables web users to easily create an account and to post short and interesting blog posts on any topic. Users can also share content from other sites or reblog interesting content found within the network.

Most brands use Tumblr together with their main company blogs to point their audience to interesting content through either of the platforms. By posting creative content on your Tumblr, other users are likely to reblog this content thus helping you to distribute it within the network and in other social networks. By including a link to your website, those who see your content will be inclined to visit your website or blog to access even more information.

Marketers can use several options to highlight content. These include the highlighted posts, the radar, the spotlight and the pinned posts. Through these content marketing options, users can pay $5 each day to have their content appear on their followers' feeds.

Google News

Google News is a portal that aggregates news pieces across the web and offers a single interface through which web users can access news in any category. The news pieces not only appear in Google News search results but also in Google organic searches.

Blog owners and content marketers can submit their content to Google News if your topic falls under one the categories on Google News. The sites added to Google News are required to purely provide current and relevant news content. Material such as how to articles, promotional copy, and advice articles or DIY are usually not accepted.

To make the most out of Google News, it is recommended that you distribute information that exhibits your expertise. Include your contact information and author profile in your news items to increase credibility. If you include links within the article be sure that it does not redirect users elsewhere other than the relevant domain. Done correctly, Google News can be an authoritative channel for content distribution to a very specific audience that subscribes to news in your niche.

Other news services that also serve as social media platforms include *Digg* and *Reddit*. These sites rely on user-generated content for current news pieces. Anyone can post news items, bookmark interesting content and share this content on other social media networks.

Foursquare

FourSquare is a location-based social media service that allows users to share their experience when they check into a business. Potential customers can also get alerts when they are nearby a business that may interest them.

This service takes advantage of the increasing use of mobile among customers who rely on their mobile devices to find locations, businesses, to shop and to make recommendations. Businesses that have a physical presence can use FourSquare for mobile content marketing. This type of marketing sends out messages about offers and available products to potential customers in the neighborhood. In turn, the potential customers can choose to check into the businesses and spread the word to those in their social network.

Flickr

Flickr is one of the largest and most robust photo-sharing platforms. The site is especially effective for businesses that market and sell a product due to it visual nature. However, any business related photos could still come in handy in making your brand visible using images.

Once you upload your photos, use targeted keywords to tag them and provide a description of the images. Flickr prohibits outright selling and promotion thus it is a good idea to simply display your compelling images and link these back to your site. You may also place your photos under the creative commons license to allow others to use these images elsewhere as long as they attribute the images to you.

Be sure to promote these images on other social networks by linking your Flickr profile to Facebook and Twitter, to your blog and other Web 2.0 services. You can also create or join a group that shares photos you are interested in. Groups offer you a targeted audience to which you can distribute your visual content and generate the relevant content.

Instagram

Instagram is a free photo sharing application for the iPhone and Android phones. It enables users to use their mobile devices to capture images and to share them across the web, more so in social media platforms. Facebook recently acquired the site and this will increase its user base.

Due to its portability, Instagram can be effective for distributing images around your brand and product. Show people the type of products you have or how they can use it. This will draw prospects to visit your product page on your website where they can obtain further details about what you have to offer.

The hashtag is a new feature for Instagram that allows you to optimize the images you capture and distribute. By using the hashtag, searchers can find related pictures. The hashtag you use for your Instagram pictures will also be searchable on Twitter if you link your account with Instagram.

Scribd

Scribd is a document-sharing platform that allows anyone to display books samples, chapters, reports and whole ebooks for other users to read. Those who read these documents can buy the whole book or share links to a report or document on other social networks and through emails.

For content marketers, Scribd provides an opportunity for sharing content with a targeted audience that will then help to further distribute the content within their own social network. Publishers can also sell their content by setting their prices; Scribd takes 20% of the revenue while the publisher keeps the remaining. If you distribute on Scribd you can choose to allow free access or encode the documents to keep readers from downloading without permission.

AdWords

Paid search can be a valuable strategy that complements your search engine optimization efforts. Running a Google Adwords campaign can help you determine the keywords that will attract greater conversions for the content in your website or blog. Well targeted and keyword rich Adwords campaign can enhance the click through rate to your site or to any domain that hosts your content.

An essential Google Adwords best practice is to use the same keywords in your ad copy and in the landing page that searchers are directed to when they click through your ad. This consistency will improve your website's Quality Score. Also, potential customers who click on your ad are likely to stay on your website longer if they find the same content on the landing page.

Facebook Advertising

Facebook advertising enables marketers to create messages that can be targeted to different and specific users based on the information on the users' profile. The Facebook profile targeting capability makes business to customer very effective especially on this platform. This is because much of the user statistics are based on personal demographics and interests. As such, you can target users based on factors such gender, age, education, geographical location or their place of work.

Facebook advertising also allows for geo-targeting that allows marketers to advertise the products based on the geographical location of the prospects. The ads enable marketers to generate 'Likes' on their company pages; this can boost the growth your Facebook network, helping you to garner prospects, who can be converted to leads for your content. Facebook advertisements are on a cost per thousand impressions or cost-per-click basis.

Twitter Advertising

The real-time nature of Twitter makes it a valuable communication and content distribution tool. However, Twitter advertising is still very limited to the larger brands with big advertising budgets. Twitter advertising is in the form of Promoted Trends or Sponsored Tweets.

Marketers pay for their Twitter messages to appear to appear in Twitter users' feeds when users search for a related keyword or hashtag. It is possible to target specific users without the need to send tweets to all your followers. Marketers can send targeted messages to users in different geographic and time zones.

For smaller marketers, Twitter is yet to offer an economically viable content marketing and advertising model. However, as the platform develops its monetization strategy, Twitter will offer a greater opportunity for real-time business to customer content marketing and advertising.

LinkedIn Advertising

Advertising on LinkedIn enables marketers to target a very specific audience that can be converted to promising leads. In the same way that advertisers use Sponsored Stories to market their Facebook pages, they can also use LinkedIn advertising to promote company and product pages. You can do this by directing users to your website or to LinkedIn company pages.

The ads on LinkedIn are typically very brief with a maximum of 25 characters for the title and 75 characters for the ad copy. In addition to using these ads to promote content in your company pages, marketers can also submit status updated about the company.

To make the most of LinkedIn advertising for your content marketing campaign, use the available targeting tool to reach the relevant audience. You can target prospects based on their industry, their career and professional interests or the LinkedIn groups they belong to. Use the Groups Statistics option to determine the level of activity in a group before targeting it.

The LinkedIn Today feature is valuable as it enables you to see the news that is widely shared across the platform and in all present industries. Through this, you can identify the type of news and content that people in your industry may be interested in. Effective LinkedIn advertising is a lucrative opportunity for business-to-business lead generation with a minimum budget of $10 a day.

HubPages

HubPages is a content sharing platform that lets you to write and distribute content in your areas of expertise. To get started in creating content on this platform you simply need to create an account and you will be assigned a URL for this account. It is important that your URL is keyword optimized to make your hubs visible to those who may be looking for your content.

 An important consideration is the capsules feature that allows you to build your hub in a way that will be interesting to readers. Make use of the photo, video and map capsule as much as you do the text capsules. These sections allow you to add dynamic content to your hubs.

HubPages attracts a lot of traffic and a high page raking and can be a beneficial source of quality inbound links. However, the amount of traffic your content attracts depends on its quality, uniqueness and relevance to your target audience. As part of your content distribution strategy, you can link your HubPages with your social media marketing efforts. This will direct your social network on Twitter, Facebook and other platforms to your hubs.

By sharing your hubs on other networks, you will generate traffic to both your HubPages and your website. This two-pronged approach enables your site and HubPages to be indexed faster and to appear on the search results page. Note that HubPages is particularly beneficial for websites focused on specific niches. Using niche specific keywords in your content and tagging your hubs appropriately will boost your content index as well as generate relevant traffic to your hubs and website.

Squidoo

Squidoo is a social media content distribution site that allows users to interact with others on the platform. The site offers features such as a link directory and polls to increase interactivity. It works based on the concept of lenses, which is simply a publishing account through which you a can distribute and market your content.

Like other article submission sites with a high page ranking, Squidoo will only publish quality content. The articles published through your lens must be well researched, interesting, informative and unique. Squidoo has many regulations in an effort to maintain the high page ranking on the search engines. Before your content is published, Squidoo will assign a lens rank index to your content before placing it in the directory and distribute it to other places such as the Squidoo online magazine.

When your lens rank drops, it will no longer appear in the Squidoo title directories. This also means that it will not show up on the search engine results page. To improve your lens rank, you can add new content to the lens, format it and then publish it again. You can also share the lens on social networks to generate traffic for it. This will serve to boost its visibility and subsequently improve on the lens rank.

Another important consideration is the number of links you can place within an article. The fewer, the better. The link filter disallows users to place more than 9 links directing to the same domain within a single article.

SlideShare

SlideShare is a free presentation forum that allows users to create short informative slide presentations that can be viewed by any web users. This is an ideal platform to reach professional audiences and those who are likely to be interested in your content and subsequently in your business. SlideShare is also a high-ranking content sharing platform that attracts up to 60 million visits each month. It also boasts 3 billion slide views each month. This means that the traffic potential for content is impressive and because the site has a high page ranking, presented content is likely to feature highly on the search engines - the right combination for content marketers.

The great thing about SlideShare is that you can promote your brand and product offering as much as you like. Unlike other content promotion platforms, users can make a sales presentation to introduce others to their products. To be effective on SlideShare it is best to offer content that is informative and interesting to your target audience. Offer insights about how your product can meet certain needs or create a presentation about something in your niche.

The platform is effective for sharing short, simple presentations. Including images and infographs in your content will boost its visual appeal. Remember to optimize your presentation by using the appropriate keywords that potential visitors are likely to use to find your information.

Importantly, add follow links that will direct readers to your website or social network pages. Include the link on the first and last slide to allow users to reach you in the event that they are impressed by your presentation. Additionally, SlidesShare allows you to embed and further distribute your presentation elsewhere such as in your website, blog and social media accounts.

<u>Other Suitable Tools For Content Distribution and Marketing Automation are:</u>

SocialMention

SocialMention is an easy to use tool for monitoring social media activity. Through this service, you can see what others are saying about you and your brand, or any topic that you have an interest in. This listening tool collects information generated by other social network users and allows you to analyze it on one interface.

When you know what people are talking about the most and where these conversations are taking place you are able to determine the type of content to create and distribute. You are also in a position to distribute this content through the right channels.

Bit.ly

Bit.ly is a URL shortener that allows you to share long links easily and in a friendly format. It also keeps a database of the links you have shortened so you do not have to keep shortening these links.

TubeMogul

TubeMogul is an online video marketing and distribution platform that helps publishers to get their videos to high-ranking video sharing platforms. The service provides video content automation and uploading to top sites including YouTube, Vimeo and others.

AMA

Article Marketing Automation services or software help in distributing articles to content directories. The best AMA services or software ensures that your articles are visible across the web as they are distribute to directories with high page rankings at the search results page.

UAW

Unique Article Wizard content can be a valuable way of creating content and automatically distributing unique articles to article directories. The process entails writing one article and then rewriting it twice to create three unique articles. Several UAW companies create these articles for marketers who can then have a constant availability of content to distribute.

7

CONTENT PERFORMANCE MEASUREMENT

When it comes to measuring the effectiveness of content, no single metric will suffice. Content performance measurement entails the use of diverse metrics and tools to determine how well you are achieving your content market goals.

Marketers measure their content performance for a number of reasons including: to enlarge the prospects and customer base, to support the overall marketing strategy, to customer and fan relationship building, brand monitoring and reputation management. It is important to measure content performance against the overriding business goals. Some important metrics to take into considerations are:

Followers

Before delving deep into other measurements, you want to determine the number of followers you have accessing and reading your current content. An important question to ask is\how many people are visiting my site to read the content here? Here, you are measuring the number of unique visitors to your site as well as return site visitors. This will tell you how visible your content is and whether you should be doing more to be noticed.

You also want to determine the level of subscription to your RSS feeds and email newsletters. This measurement will help you understand the numbers of people who are engaging with your content at some level. Admittedly, the number of subscriptions does not tell you how many loyal customers you have. Some people may only be following you to get information about a product or to take advantage of a discounted offers and promotions.

Consumption Levels

As the name suggests, consumption metrics tells you how people are engaging with your content. Important considerations to take here are factors such as how often how people download your content, the number of page views and site views you receive. Tools such as Google Analytics and YouTube Insights can help you measure consumption metrics effectively.

Several questions you can ask in measuring content consumption are:

What is the number of times that content downloaded or viewed?

How long did user stay on the page or site viewing this content and how much did they read or view?

What type of action did site visitors take upon reading or viewing the content? Did they provide their personal information to receive email newsletters or did they subscribe to your channel or blog RSS feed?

Did site visitors distribute the content to their social network, including family, friends and colleagues?

After reading one article or viewing one video, did site visitors follow other links to related content? Did they finally end the process by making an inquiry with you or ordered the product?

What type of interest if any did you content generate? Did the message become viral, attract media attention, and promote more click-through rates or impressions.

Social media has made it more feasible for new marketers to measure consumptions using proxies. Proxy metrics are simple, immediate metrics that can guide you in determining your initial success in your content marketing strategy. Some quick proxy metrics are Facebook likes, LinkedIn shares, retweets and @mentions, comments link backs and the number of times your posts are reblogged elsewhere.

These immediate and small-scale metrics will help you determine the progress you are making in specific areas of your content marketing. You will find that the 10 likes in a day on Facebook shows more progress in terms of content consumption than 10 likes in a month.

Impact

As a marketer, you are certainly in competition with other businesses. Customers are becoming particular about the types of brands they choose to engage with and these brands have to be making an impact on them.

An important metric to measure is the impact your content is having on your audience and other web users, in comparison to your competitors. Essentially, the impact metric is a competitive analysis. As you measure your impact, consider this:

Are clients mentioning your brand or products?

How often do they do this and are the mentions positive or negative?

How are you engaging with these mentions?

What are your customers saying about your competition and how is this impacting your business?

Has your content impacted how people perceive your brand? That is, have brand sentiments changed over time?

Conversion Rates and Revenues

Conversion rates and revenues seem to be the predominant factors that measure the success of content marketing strategy. High conversion rates do not always translate to increased revenues. The conversion rate is calculated as the percentage of the number of site visitors who make a full conversion. The conversion could be in terms of a lead or a lead. So for example if your ecommerce site receives 50 visits and 10 of these culminate to a sale, then the conversion rate would be 20%.

I.e. conversion rate= Number of sales or leads divided by the number of site visits

However, measuring content performance based on conversion rates and revenues is no straightforward. This is especially true when it comes to conversions that are less sales-oriented. Just because a site visitor converts into a regular recipient of your new letter does not mean that they will purchase anything from you other than just consuming information.

Additionally, another reason why your conversion rates may seem higher at some point could be a decrease in site visitors and a gentle rather than a drastic fall in sales. As such when using conversion rates to measure content performance it is important to consider other factors. Instead of concluding that your conversion rate is high, determine what has contributed to this spike.

On a similar note, it is advisable to look at the channels that are boosting your conversion rate. How are people gaining access to your content, before they make the decision to purchase or subscribe to your product offering? Understanding these channels will help you determine those that are working and those that should be improved to enhance your content marketing strategy.

You also want to divide your audience into unique visitors and returning visitors. Which of these two groups is generating greater conversion rates and why? You might note that changes to your content are more likely to impact new visitors than existing one. New site visitors are more influenced by the perception they have of your brand.

Existing visitors are more concerned about content and product quality, as well as the brand itself. Some factors to consider when measuring content performance with conversion rates and revenues in mind:

Did the content marketing trigger any purchases? Having links to products and product pages will help you measure this effectively.

How much of a product are people ordering, in terms of their spend rate and the quantity?

How often are content consumers converting into content or product buyers?

Tools For Measuring Content Performance

1. Google Analytics

Google Analytics is a free tool that allows you to set up goals and measure various metrics pertaining to your content. Some of these include:

a) Content consumption: number of downloads, page views and shared content

b) Channels that are generating inbound traffic to your site

c) Keywords used to find your content

d) Conversion rates

To get started with Google Analytics, you need to set up a Google account. The Goals and Conversions tab allows you to create goals for your website and then track the metrics that impact on your content performance. Once you create a goal, the next step is to include a measurable metric, such as social value when measuring social conversion rates.

Setting up this goal and including the appropriate measurable value will show help you determine the effectiveness of your content marketing and social marketing in boosting social conversions.

One a similar note the Assisted Social Conversions tab will show you the number of conversions that have take place in terms of unique visitors and returning visitors. The Social Sources report shows the social media channels that serve as a source of inbound traffic to your site. The tool also shows how these social media users are interacting with your bran and content.

Other metrics you can measure and track with Google Analytics with regard to your content are:

URL: By setting up this Goal, you are able to track site visits to particular pages on your website. This will help you see how people are accessing and engaging with specific content. Google Analytics allows you to measure the impact of the content on each page. Simply create a goals by include the URL that directs to a specific page and then track how site visitors are interacting with each page.

Time On Site: This Goal helps you to determine the amount of time that site visitors spend viewing the content on your site. You can specify the time in terms of number of hours, minutes or even seconds. As seen, previously the time site victors spend looking at your site content can be a good measure of their engagement and consumption of content.

Pages visit: Creating this Goal will help you determine the level of consumption for you website. You will not only track the number of times a user visits your site, but also the number of times they view other related materials on the site.

Events: The Events Goal shows you the type of activity site visitors engage in when they come across your content. Do they download it, view a video or do they leave the site? This is an important Goal to measure to understand the level of engagement users are having with your content when they access it. You will also know if more needs to be done to retain visitors on the site and to prompt them to take a certain action.

2. Social Mention

Social Mention is a valuable tool that enables you to listen to what your clients and audience is saying about your brand. By monitoring what is being said, you can begin to determine the impact your content is having online. Essentially, Social Mention is a search engine that allows you to type in a query or a keyword to locate information and mentions in blogs and micro-blogs, new sites, video and audio sharing platforms. There is no limit to the type of parameters you can use to find where your content or brand is mentioned.

3. Pin Reach

Pin Reach enables you to determine your influence on the micro blogging and image-sharing platform, Pinterest. Once you log into your Pin Reach account, you will access the dashboard that reveals your Pin Reach score. The score is an aggregate of several activities including repins, your number of followers and the number of people you follow, likes and comments and your boards.

Pin Reach also features four primary tabs. The Analytics button represents your trends including your score, how often your pins are repined and how popular your boards are. The Boards button offers analytics about the content in each of your bards including followers, comments, likes and repins. The Pins tab shows your 10 most popular pins and the Influential Followers shows the most influential users on Pinterest that are following you.

4. Klout

Social media influence is controversial yet tools such as Klout are still valuable in helping you to determine the impact your message is in the social-sphere. Klout measures your social influence as a factor of your capacity to trigger action in your social network. Your Klout Score is determined by three factors: true reach, amplification, and network impact.

True Reach: This is a measure of the number of people impacted by your content. Klout focuses on the actual number of people who read your message and as such share or respond to it obviously spam does not count and is in fact filtered out.

Amplification: This is a measure of the level of your impact. What do people do with your message or content when they receive it? Do they respond to your call-to-action to share and distribute the information? The more people distribute your content, the higher your amplifications score.

Network: This indicates the type of people you are connected to as part of your true reach. It is a measure of the influence that those in your social network have. Do top influencers engage with your content by sharing it or responding to it? If so, this boosts your Network score.

CONCLUSION

Throughout this book I have shown you that content is the key to everything. It brings traffic, converts customers and in the age of web 2.0, allows us to have direct 2-way interactions with our customers. The key however to using content effectively is to be smart, innovative and strategic with the use of your digital content. The internet is an ever evolving web of digital marketing content and if you don't plan cleverly around what kind of material you place where and when then you will not maximize your online presence and income-generating potential.

Whether you choose to use text, images or video content or a combination of all, the key is to plan strategically and to ensure that the content you provide is interesting, creative and provides value to the consumer. I have covered a number of aspects from content creation to optimization and distribution and from free to premium or original to curated content. I hope you have found this book useful and that you use some of the tips I have provided in your own campaigns. I would however also encourage you to be creative and find a content strategy that works well for you.

Remember that content is everything and an online marketing strategy in today's digital world that doesn't consider content as the number one item when it comes to campaign planning is a strategy that is doomed to fail.

If you enjoyed this book, I would appreciate if you could share your feedback with other Amazon readers. If you have any questions related to the topics discussed in this book, please do not hesitate to send me an email to globalndigital@gmail.com.

As I continue my research, I will make updates to this book. As you already know, I will simply do this by adding to my book and uploading the new book to Amazon. However that means that you will not get the benefit of my new research. Please send me an email to globalndigital@gmail.com so I know that you are interested in receiving updated copies of this book as soon as they are released.

Gabriela Taylor

ABOUT THE AUTHOR

Gabriela Taylor is an internationally educated Global Online Marketing Strategist and Consultant who's worked with some of the world's biggest brands in Telecommunications, Retail, Lifestyle and Advertising.

A recognized expert and specialist in Social Networking, Mobile Marketing and Search Engine Optimization she is fluent in 7 languages, has lived and worked in many countries throughout the world and has experience of implementing successful web-presence strategies for both startup and large established organizations.

She is the founder of Global N' Digital, a consultancy firm specializing in Online Marketing services and Cross-Cultural business practices around the world and has also published several industry related books.

Socialize To Monetize

Engaging Your Online Community Across
Multiple Social Media Platforms

GABRIELA TAYLOR

The Ultimate Guide To Building
And Marketing Your Online Business

Discover The Free Tools & Top Tips That Will Kick
Start, Grow And Maximize Your Online Business

GABRIELA TAYLOR

The Ultimate Guide To Building And Marketing Your Business With ...

Google

A Step By Step Guide To Unlocking The Power Of Google Tools And Maximizing Your Online Potential

GABRIELA TAYLOR

From Local To Global

TAKING YOUR ONLINE BUSINESS TO NEW MARKETS

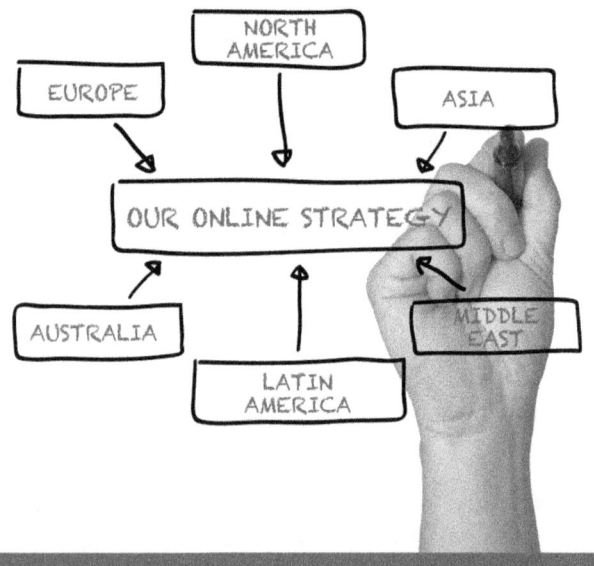

GABRIELA TAYLOR

The Ultimate Guide To Marketing
Your Business With...

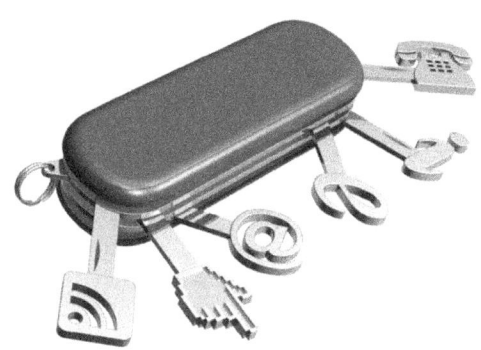

A Practical Toolkit To Unlock The Web's
Latest Social Networking Phenomenon

GABRIELA TAYLOR

The Ultimate Guide To Marketing Your Business With…

Using Tumblr To Leverage Social Buzz And Develop A Brand Awareness Strategy For Your Business

GABRIELA TAYLOR